Contents

Exploring the Earth

You probably know though you would never guess it from looking around you, that the Earth is round, like an orange. It spins as it travels round the Sun.

A flat map of the world can never be quite right. The shapes of the countries and the oceans have to be changed to make them fit on the page: like trying to flatten out orange peel.

The only kind of map that shows the shapes as they really are is a **globe.** How is it different from a map?

Globes often have clock faces showing different times on them. What do you think these are for?

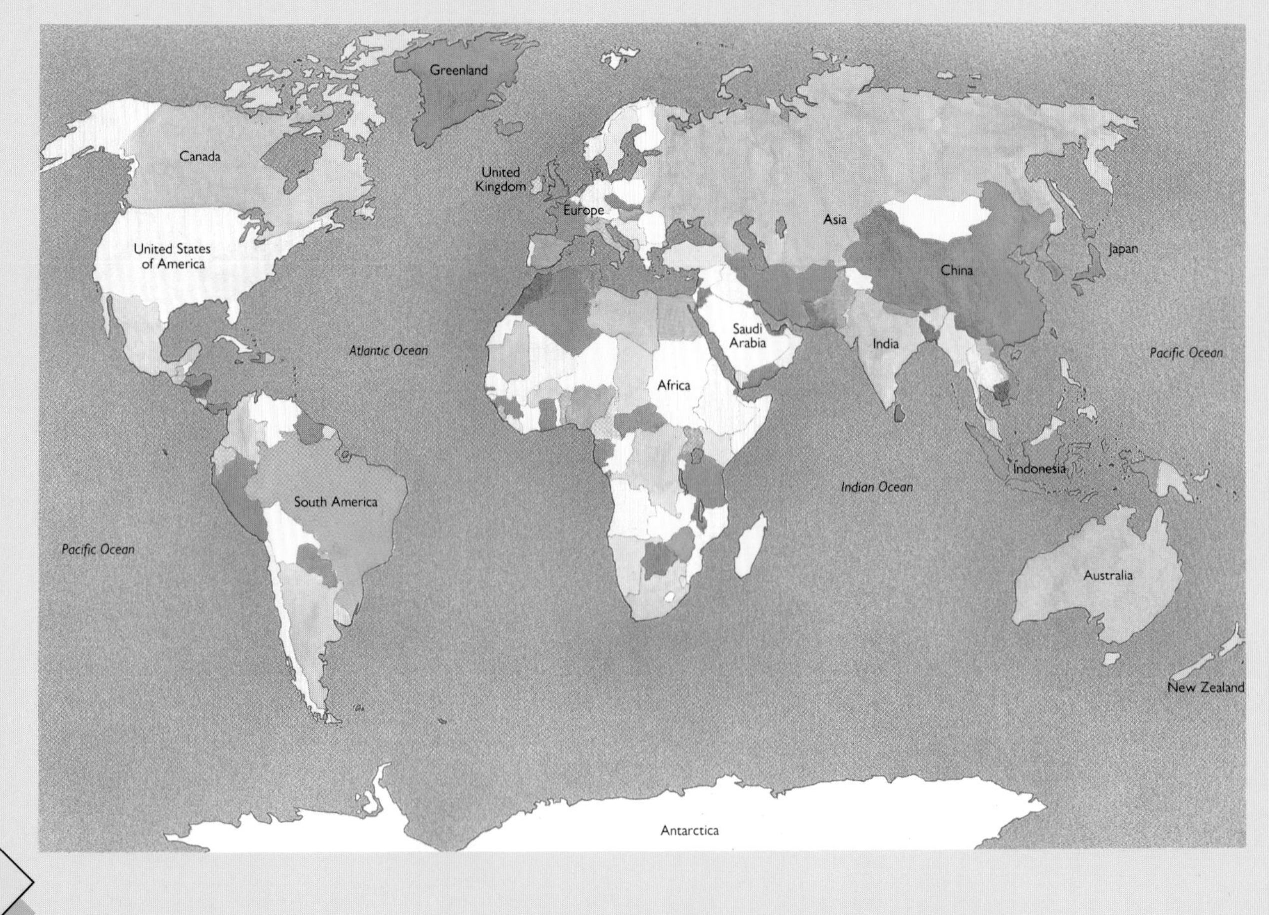

If you have a globe at school, use it to explore the Earth. You can travel with your eyes and your fingers.

Look for places you know.
Look for Britain.

Plan a journey. Trace the route to Africa (decide which part you want to visit). Then travel on to India, and then to North and South America.

Look for countries you have been to on holiday, or to see relatives and friends. Can you work out which route you took?

Where do you find hot countries on the globe? Where are the cold countries?

How much of the world is sea?

Find the North Pole and the South Pole. Find the Equator.

Looking at the Earth

This is what part of the **Earth** looks like, from Space. The colours are not the real ones.

Which countries can you recognize?

Can you guess from the photographs what the weather is like in Britain? Or in France?

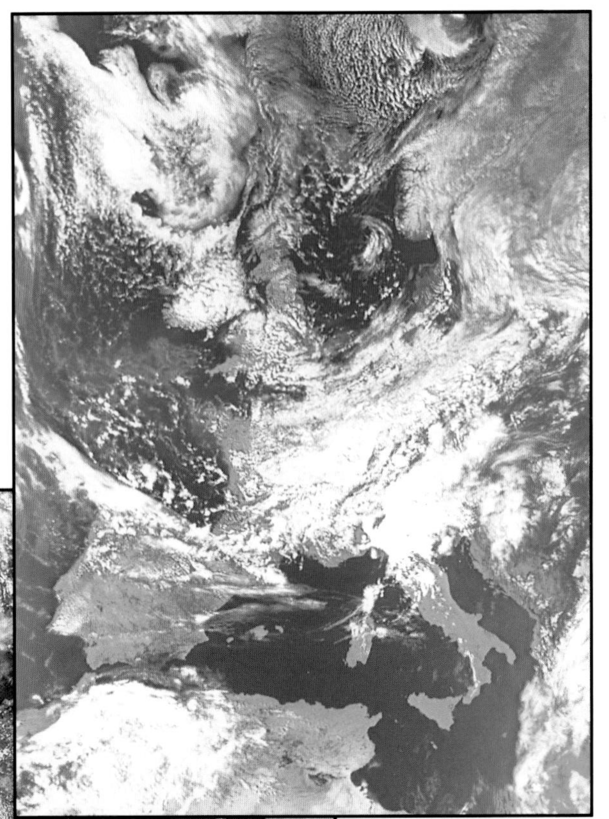

Photographs like these are taken from **satellites** going round the Earth.

Wow! Satellite pictures can show swarms of locusts on their way to attack crops. Spy satellites can take pictures of armies on the move.

You can see a weather satellite in this photograph. It runs on energy collected by solar panels.

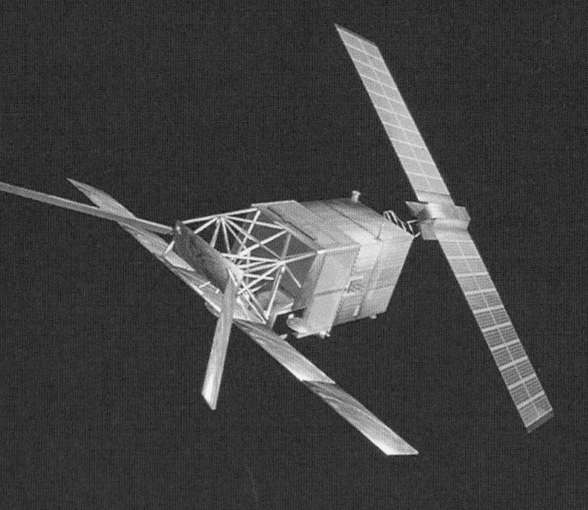

Wow!

Danger! Flying rubbish! An American space shuttle had its window cracked by a flake of paint travelling at thousands of kilometres an hour.

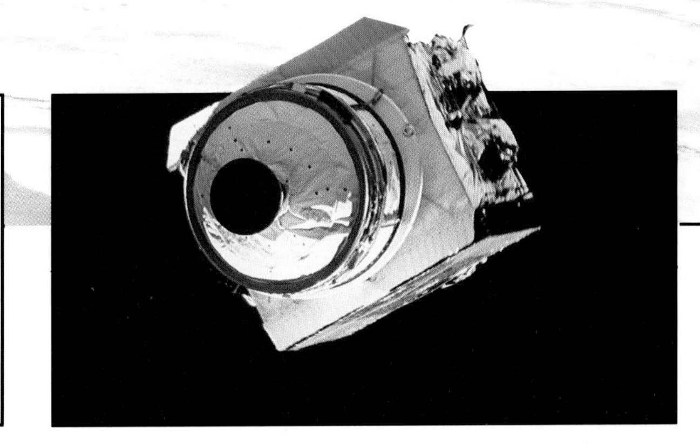

What happens to old satellites, pieces of rockets, and rubbish from space stations? There are more than 8,000 large bits of rubbish in Space. Some people think that the Earth might one day look like the planet Saturn, with a ring of rubbish instead of dust round it.

This is a communications satellite shortly after being launched from a space shuttle. Its **solar panels** are still folded up. It may relay television programmes or telephone calls from one part of the Earth to another, or messages from Earth to a space station.

What time of year is it?

Imagine you had landed on **Earth** after a long trip into Outer Space. Your starship docks close to home – you know exactly where you are, but you have lost all sense of time. You do not even know what time of year it is. How will you guess? What clues will you look for?

Shadows

You know you can use shadows to help you guess what time of day it is. Did you know that shadows also change at different times of the year?

What makes shadows long or short? You could try this for yourself with a torch. Shine it at small objects, from different angles. What do you notice?

Here are some pictures to help you think of clues. What time of year do you think it is, in each one? How did you work it out?

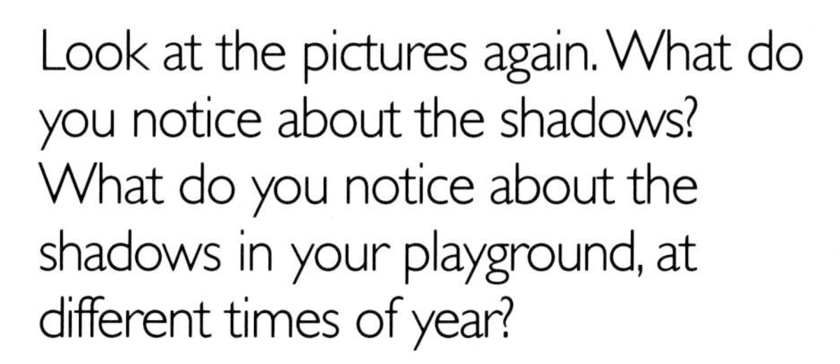

Look at the pictures again. What do you notice about the shadows? What do you notice about the shadows in your playground, at different times of year?

The Sun, the Moon, and the stars

Q What are stars?

A Stars are suns, like our Sun, billions of kilometres away. Our Sun is much brighter because it is so much nearer.

Q What is the Sun?

A The Sun is a ball of very hot gas – mostly hydrogen.

Q Why can't we see the stars in the daytime?

A We can – we can see the Sun, our nearest star. When it shines, it lights up billions of tiny pieces of dust and drops of water in the sky. This makes the sky shine more brightly than the other stars, so we can't see them.

Q What is the Moon?

A The Moon is a small world, going round the **Earth.** It has no light of its own. It shines because it is reflecting light from the Sun.

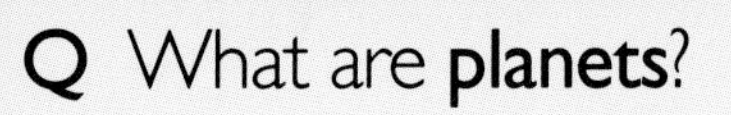

Q What are **planets**?

A Planets look rather like stars in the night sky, but they gradually change their position. They are not really like stars – they are worlds going round the Sun, like the Earth is.

What is the universe like?

Aristotle

For many hundreds of years scientists have been studying the Sun, Moon, and **planets** in the sky.

The Greek **philosopher**, Aristotle, lived over 2000 years ago. He thought that the Universe looked like this. The **Earth** is in the centre, and the Sun, Moon, and planets went round the Earth.

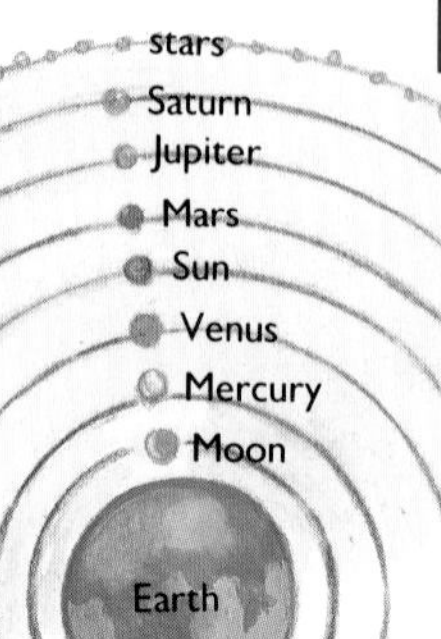

Other people thought that the universe was shaped like this. Rain was water trickling through holes in the sky. If you went too close to the edge of the world you could fall off.

The Sun rode on a chariot. It went into the sea every night, and was re-born in the morning.

Some people thought that the Earth was held up by elephants.

The facts

The Earth is round, like a ball. It is always spinning. Someone at the Equator may not realize it, but they are travelling at about 16,100 kilometres an hour.

The Earth takes 24 hours to spin round once.

It spins just over 365 times a year.

The Earth takes a year to travel round the Sun.

The Moon goes round the Earth, at the same time as both of them are going round the Sun.

The Solar System

The Solar System is the name for the Sun and **planets** that go round it. Planets do not give out light, like the stars do, but they reflect light from the Sun.

Mercury is the closest to the Sun. It is the hottest planet.

Venus has a temperature hot enough to melt lead and its clouds rain acid. It is an extreme example of the 'greenhouse effect'.

Earth is the only planet in the Solar System thought to have life on it. We call it the blue planet. Why do you think it looks blue?

Mars is called the red planet – it has red soil, pink sky and two moons.

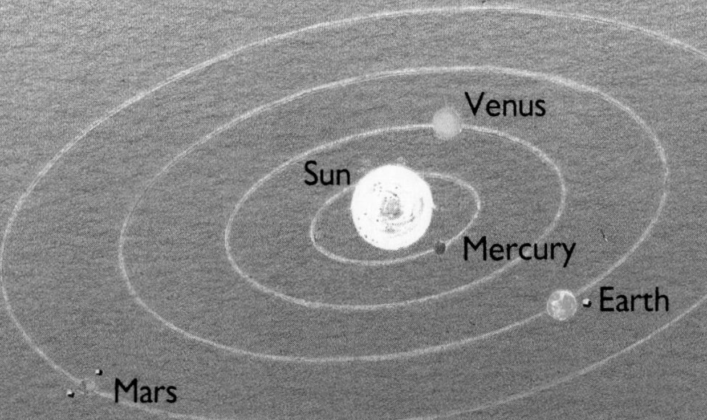

Jupiter is the largest planet, a thousand times bigger than the Earth. Jupiter is mostly gas and liquid. It has no hard surface for a spacecraft to land on.

Saturn has rings of billions of small rocks around it. Like Jupiter, it is mostly gas and liquid.

Uranus has rings like Saturn, but much fainter. We first saw these when the space probe *Voyager 2* flew past it in 1986.

Neptune is a blue-green planet discovered in 1846. *Voyager 2* took three years to get from Uranus to Neptune, and flew past it in 1989.

Pluto is a small cold planet which was only discovered in 1930. It has one moon, Charon. We know very little about Pluto.

Jupiter

Saturn

Uranus

Neptune

Pluto

True or false?

Many of our ideas are influenced by what we read and what we see on television. Sometimes it is hard to know which things are true and which are false.

Try these. Are they true or false? The answers are upside down on this page.

1 Twelve people have been to the Moon. Some left cars there.

2 Every day, 15,000 tonnes of rock and dust from Outer Space falls to **Earth.**

3 Captain Kirk, Mr Spock, and the crew of the Starship Enterprise have travelled into Outer Space.

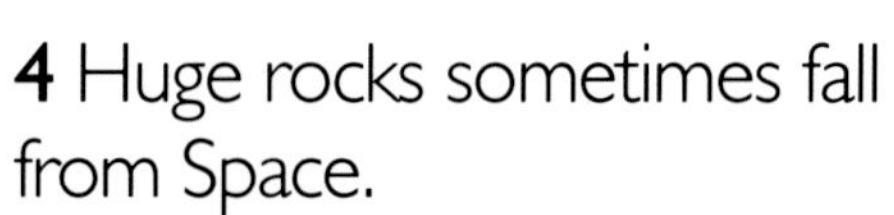

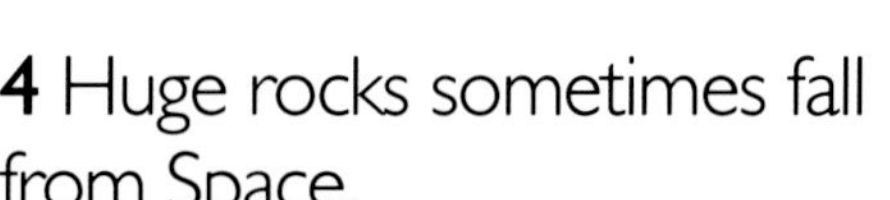

4 Huge rocks sometimes fall from Space.

5 Saturn is the only **planet** that has rings.

6 Our Solar System has thousands of little planets in it.

7 A cow has jumped over the Moon.

Answers

1 True. In the 1960s and 1970s the Americans sent six Apollo missions to the Moon, with two people on each. Some missions took lunar rovers (not really cars) and left them behind. There's also an unmanned Soviet car there.

2 True, but most burns up before it reaches the ground.

3 False. Only in 'Star Trek'!

4 True, they are called meteors. This crater in Arizona, USA was caused by a giant meteor.

5 False. Jupiter, Uranus and Neptune all have rings but only faint ones.

6 True. They are called asteroids. Most are just large rocks but some are several kilometres across.

7 False. This is just a nursery rhyme.

Time and the Sun

Even before people knew how the Sun and the **Earth** move in Space, they used the Sun to help them tell the time. They looked at the position of shadows on the ground, and worked out the time from these.

How did they do this? Try looking at shadows on a sunny day. Do they stay in the same place all the time? Or do they change?

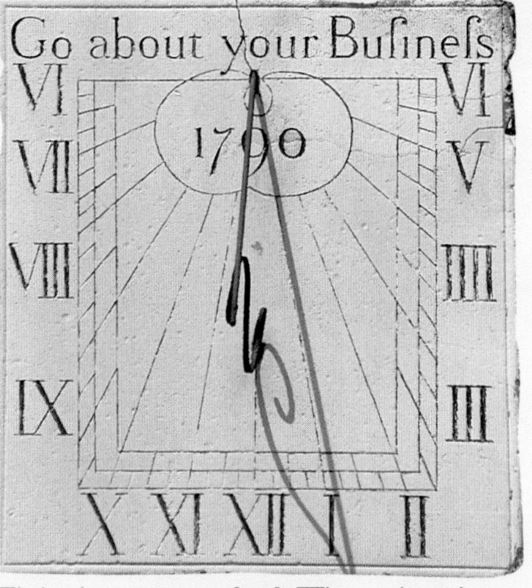

This is a **sundial.** The shadow shows what time it is.

What time of day do you think it is in these pictures?

What clues do you use?

Wow!

In summer, the Sun stays in the sky longer and daylight lasts until very late. In summer in the far north, the Sun sets so late and rises so early that it is light almost all night. People sometimes call this part of the world 'The Land of the Midnight Sun'. At mid-winter, darkness lasts almost all day.

Day and night – guessing the time

When you wake up, how do you know if it is day or night?

What if you kept your eyes closed? What are the clues which would tell you what time of day it is?

What are night sounds like?

What are day sounds like?

We asked some blind children: 'How do you guess what the time is?' Here are some of the things they said:

'Some of us can see whether it's light or dark, so we know if it's night or day.'

'It's warmer in the morning than in the afternoon.'

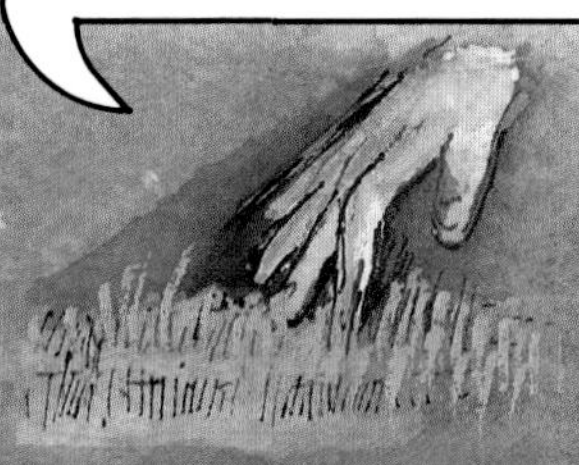

'The grass gets damp in the evenings.'

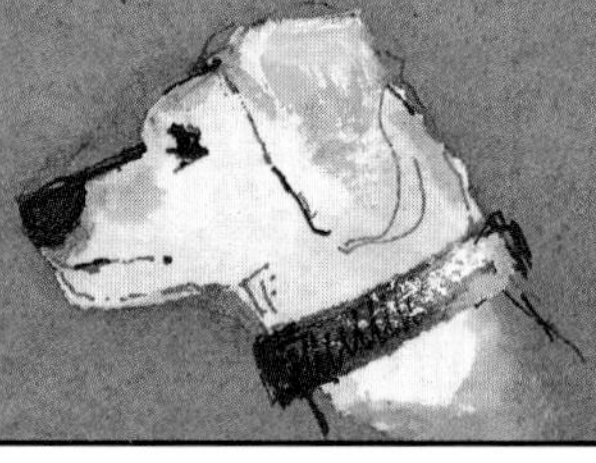

'My tummy tells me when it's lunch time!'

'I can tell when it's morning and time to get up because my dog wakes me up, wanting his breakfast.'

'I can always tell when it's Sunday lunchtime the whole street smells of roast meat!'

'The air smells fresh in the morning and stale at the end of the day.'

'I can hear owls at night, where I live.'

'The cockerel at the farm opposite crows every morning.'

'The birds make a lot of noise in the morning and in the afternoon. They don't make any noise at night.'

'When I wake up in the night, it's quiet. I know it's morning when I hear my Mum in the kitchen and I can smell breakfast cooking.'

'I can hear cars in the morning and afternoon when it's rush-hour.'

What clues can you think of, to help you tell the time?

The Sun and the Moon

A story from Guadeloupe

The Sun had never seen the night, and was curious to know what it was like. One evening, instead of going to bed as usual, the Sun stayed up to have a look.

When it got dark, he was amazed to see the sky full of stars and the Moon shining brightly. Everything looked lovely.

However, the Moon wasn't at all happy to see the Sun at a time when he should have been in bed. Night time was the Moon's time, not the Sun's. The Moon decided to put a stop to the Sun's interest in darkness, so that he would never want to stay up and see it again.

The Moon asked the clouds to help him. Together, they made mysterious shadows, and what had been trees turned into creepy shapes like witches. All the dogs began to howl and thousands of bats flew around. In no time at all the Sun decided that night time wasn't so nice after all and he fled to the safety of his bed.

From that day on the Sun has been happy to shine in the day and leave the night to the Moon.

Night-life

We usually think of night as a time when we are asleep. But there is a lot of activity at night. Think about people who have to work at night.

Hospital

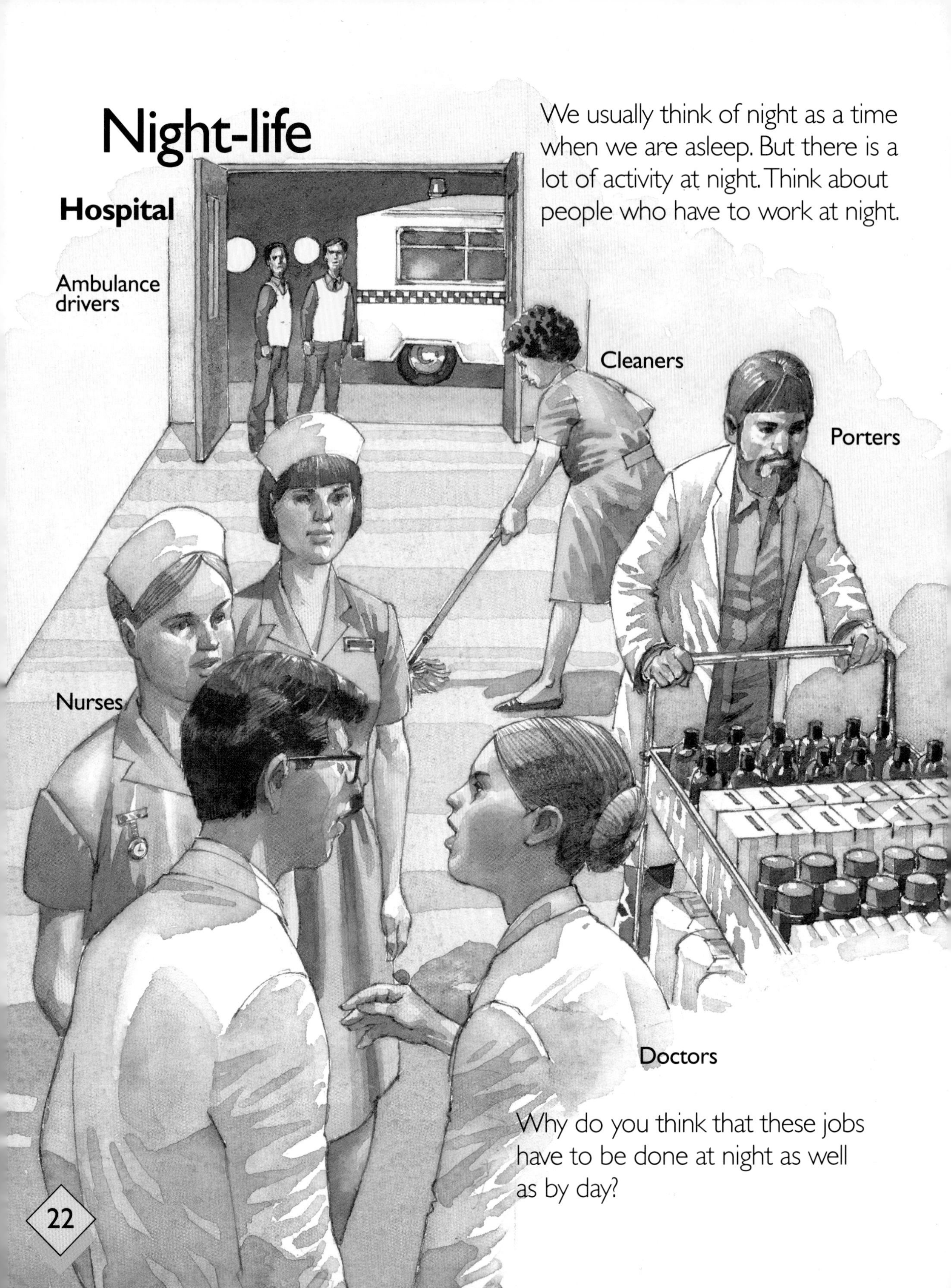

Why do you think that these jobs have to be done at night as well as by day?

Parliament

MPs often stay up all night to finish discussing something. This isn't surprising – they don't start until three in the afternoon.

What other places can you think of, where people work all night? What are they doing?

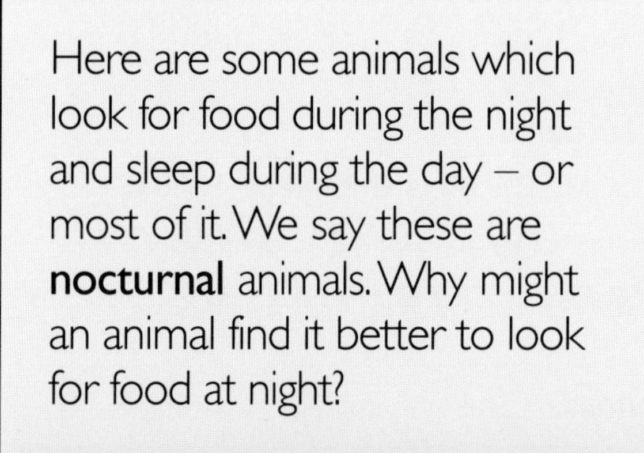

Here are some animals which look for food during the night and sleep during the day – or most of it. We say these are **nocturnal** animals. Why might an animal find it better to look for food at night?

Glossary

Earth
The Earth is the name given to the planet on which we live.

Globe
A ball-shaped map of the world.

Nocturnal
Nocturnal animals are awake during the night and sleep during the day.

Philosopher
A person who tries, by thinking and arguing, to find out the truth about the world and the way in which people live.

Planet
The word planet is usually used for the nine huge satellites of the Sun. They all follow different paths around the Sun. Lots of other planets travel round the Sun as well, but they are much smaller and are generally called asteroids.

This is the planet Saturn.

Satellite
A satellite is something which travels through Space, round and round the Earth, or around another planet or star. The Moon is a satellite of the Earth, and the Earth is a satellite of the Sun. Some countries send up satellites using rockets. These satellites are machines which let people send and collect information from other countries.

Solar panel
A solar panel is designed to trap the energy of sunlight and turn it into electricity or heat energy.

Sundial
A sundial is a kind of clock that uses sunlight to show the time. You read the time by looking at the position of the shadow thrown by a pointer onto a flat plate, which is marked out in hours. Of course, you can only use a sundial if the Sun is actually shining – otherwise there isn't any shadow

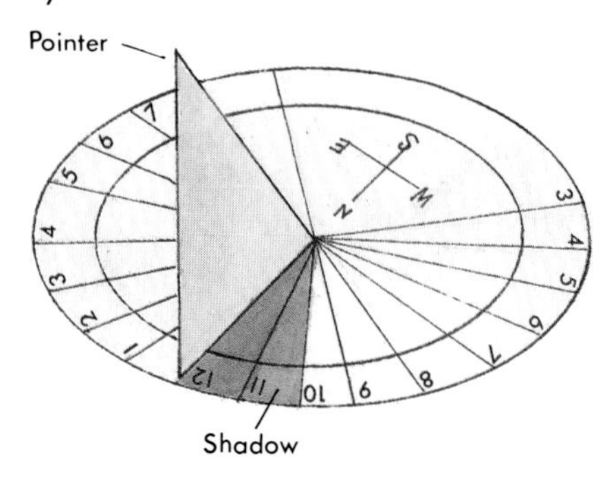